©2021 Simple Kid Press.

Cover and interior design by Simple Kid Press Group

ISBN: 9798409587864

MW00950276

SCAN ME

WOULD YOU LIKE
A **FREE** PRINTABLE
ACTIVITY FOR KIDS?

OR go to
http://bit.ly/
simplekidpress

OTHER TITLES AVAILABLE:

Blank sticker collecting albums

Scene Sticker Albums:

THIS BOOK BELONGS TO

_____

_____

TABLE OF CONTENTS

MY DINOSAUR STICKERS

MY UNICORN STICKERS

MY ANIMAL STICKERS

MY BIRD STICKERS

MY DOG STICKERS

MY CAT STICKERS

MY CAR STICKERS

MY PRINCESS STICKERS

MY SUPERHERO STICKERS

MY ROBOT STICKERS

MY CHRISTMAS STICKERS

MY EASTER STICKERS

MY THANKSGIVING STICKERS

MY HALLOWEEN STICKERS

MY SPACE STICKERS

MY MONSTER STICKERS

MY FOOD STICKERS

MY INSECT STICKERS

MY SUMMER STICKERS

MY WINTER STICKERS

MY SPRING STICKERS

MY AUTUMN STICKERS

MY BIRTHDAY STICKERS

MY CUTE STICKERS

MY AWESOME STICKERS

MY SCARY STICKERS

MY BIG STICKERS

MY TINY STICKERS

MY U6LY STICKERS

MY _____ STICKERS

MY _____ STICKERS

MY _____ STICKERS

MY _____ STICKERS

MY _____ STICKERS

MY _____ STICKERS

MY _____ STICKERS

MY _____ STICKERS

Made in the USA
Las Vegas, NV
13 December 2024

14232072R00026